# Mustangs

# The Child's World®

Published by The Child's World®
1980 Lookout Drive • Mankato, MN 56003-1705
800-599-READ • www.childsworld.com

Acknowledgments
The Child's World®: Mary Berendes, Publishing Director
The Design Lab: Design
Jody Jensen Shaffer: Editing
Red Line Editorial: Photo Research

Photo credits
Daburke/Dreamstime.com: 20; Dennis Donohue/Shutterstock.com: cover, 1; DmytroKobzar/iStock.com: 19; Eric Isselee/Shutterstock.com: 22-23; Joe Belanger/Shutterstock.com: rope; justasc/Shutterstock.com: 6; mariait/Shutterstock.com: 5; Randy Harris Photography/iStock.com: 16; St.MarieLtd./iStock.com: 12, 15; sunsinger/Shutterstock.com: 9; through-my-lens/iStock.com: 11; Vaclav Volrab/Shutterstock.com: horseshoes

ISBN 9781626870055
LCCN 2013947284

Printed in the United States of America
Mankato, MN
December, 2013
PA02195

## ABOUT THE AUTHOR

*Pamela Dell is the author of more than fifty books for young people. She likes writing about four-legged animals as well as insects, birds, famous people, and interesting times in history. She has published both fiction and nonfiction books and has also created several interactive computer games for kids. Pamela divides her time between Los Angeles, where the weather is mostly warm and sunny all year, and Chicago, where she loves how wildly the seasons change every few months.*

# CONTENTS

Horses Running Free. . . . . . . . . . . . . . . . . . . . . . . . . 4

What Do Mustangs Look Like? . . . . . . . . . . . . . . . 7

Newborn Mustangs. . . . . . . . . . . . . . . . . . . . . . . . 10

Mustangs in History . . . . . . . . . . . . . . . . . . . . . . 13

What Are Mustangs Like? . . . . . . . . . . . . . . . . . . 17

Mustangs at Work. . . . . . . . . . . . . . . . . . . . . . . . 18

Mustangs Today . . . . . . . . . . . . . . . . . . . . . . . . . 21

Body Parts of a Horse . . . . . . . . . . . . . . . 22

To Find Out More . . . . . . . . . . . . . . . . . 23

Glossary . . . . . . . . . . . . . . . . . . . . . . . . 24

Index . . . . . . . . . . . . . . . . . . . . . . . . . . 24

# Horses Running Free

A thundering sound fills the air. Dust rises from the ground. A herd of horses is galloping across the plain. No one owns these horses. They are free. They are mustangs!

Mustangs are free-running horses of western North America. These horses do not have an easy life. No one takes care of them. No one finds them food or water. They must take care of themselves. That is why these horses are so smart and strong.

Mustangs are often called "wild" horses. But an even better word is **feral**. Wild animals have always been wild. They have never been owned by anyone. But feral animals are people's pets that got loose. Mustangs came from horses people owned. Some of the horses got loose. They formed herds. They had babies. Over time, the horses got used to living on their own.

*These wild mustangs are running at sunset.*

# What Do Mustangs Look Like?

Mustangs came from a mix of horse **breeds**. They come in all shapes and colors. Most of them are small. They have thick, heavy bodies and big heads. Their backs are short. Their legs are short and strong.

A horse's height is measured from the **withers** to the ground. Most mustangs are 56 to 60 inches (142 to 152 centimeters) tall. A horse's height is also measured in hands.

A hand is 4 inches (10 centimeters). Most mustangs stand 14 to 15 hands high. Some are as small as 13 hands or as big as 16 hands. For their size, mustangs are fairly heavy. Most weigh 750 to 1,000 pounds (340 to 454 kilograms).

> Mustangs that live free often have scars. They get cuts and scrapes. Sometimes they get in fights with other mustangs.

> "Mustang" makes people think of something fast and wild. The name has been used for a fighter plane, a sports car, and sports teams.

*Mustangs come in all sorts of colors and patterns.*

You can find mustangs in just about every color and pattern. Many are **dun** or **roan**. Others are white, black, brown, **bay**, **chestnut**, or other colors. Some have splashes of white on their faces or legs. Others have small spots or big patches of color.

Mustangs' tails are set low on their bodies. Their manes are long. Sometimes their manes grow long enough to reach their legs.

Mustangs' hooves are hard. These horses can walk on rocky ground without getting hurt. They hardly ever have the leg and foot problems other horses have.

**Free-running mustangs often have lots of hair. It keeps them warm in rain, snow, and wind.**

*You can see the variety of patterns and colors mustangs can have in this picture.*

# Newborn Mustangs

In the wild, mustangs live in herds. A herd might have several **mares** and their **foals**. The herd is led by a **stallion**. He is the foals' father. Mustang herds move around a lot. The mares give birth quickly. The foals can run soon after they are born.

Mustangs take good care of their foals. At first, the foals drink only their mothers' milk. As they grow, they start eating grass and other plants. They learn how to stay alive. They learn how to get along with other mustangs. Most foals stay with their herd for one to two years. Then they leave to find herds of their own.

In the wild, many foals are born during the winter. In cold areas, the foals have thick, shaggy coats. The thick hair keeps them warm.

*This young mustang foal lives in Wyoming.*

# Mustangs in History

When Europeans arrived, North America had no horses. But the Europeans brought lots of them. Spanish, French, and English settlers brought different kinds. Some of the horses got loose. Native Americans caught some of them. But others were never caught. They became feral. These feral horses gathered into herds.

Some herds of mustangs still have mostly Spanish blood. They did not mix as much with other breeds. They are some of the most beautiful mustangs.

Some herds had mostly Spanish horses. Others had different breeds. The babies were mixes of breeds. Over time, other settlers' horses kept getting loose. These newcomers mixed with the feral horses, too.

Feral mustangs faced many dangers. But they were smart. They learned how to live in the wild. They were watchful, brave, and fast. And they had few animal enemies. Their numbers grew quickly.

*These mustangs may be descended from a number of different breeds.*

By the 1800s, everyone in the West was after the mustangs. Ranchers wanted them for saddle horses and cow ponies. Native Americans wanted them, too. Feral horses had to be taught to carry riders. People often taught them in hard, cruel ways. But these horses often kept their wild spirit. They tried to buck riders off. Sometimes they ran away—even years later.

In the early 1900s, the U.S. had about 2 million wild mustangs. People thought that was too many. They killed mustangs to get rid of them. By 1970, there were only about 17,000 mustangs left.

But some people worked hard to save the mustangs. They passed laws against killing them. They set aside areas where mustangs could live free. They kept track of how many horses these areas had. Sometimes an area had too many. Earlier, the extra horses would have been killed. Now the government started finding people who would adopt them.

**Many people thought mustangs were pests. The mustangs ate grasses that cattle could eat. People even hunted the horses for sport.**

*This pack of mustangs has plenty of space to run around.*

# What Are Mustangs Like?

Living in the wild has made mustangs smart! But they are different from other horses. Most horses grow up around people. Feral mustangs are not used to people. They are used to being free. They try to stay away from danger. People need to make friends with them gently. Being mean to mustangs makes them want to fight back. It makes them not trust people.

Once mustangs trust people, they make wonderful pets. They are strong, brave, and friendly. They do not need to be fussed over. They work hard to please people. But they still have minds of their own!

Mustangs often live to be 30 years old. That is old for a horse!

*This wild mustang is watching the photographer carefully.*

# Mustangs at Work

Old paintings and pictures show mustangs at work. These horses carried Plains Indians on buffalo hunts. They helped ranchers herd sheep and cattle.

Today, mustangs make excellent saddle horses and cow ponies. Their short backs and great strength help them carry heavy loads. Mustangs are used for trail riding, camping, and rodeos. They do not appear very often in horse shows. But some people train them for jumping and other **contests**.

Extra mustangs are still being removed from government land. People have given thousands of these horses new homes. First the horses must be "gentled." That means getting them used to people—gently! Once they trust people, they can learn their new jobs. Adopted mustangs have done well at all kinds of jobs.

> **Some people ride mustangs in *gymkhana* (jim-KAH-nuh). Gymkhana games and races are fun for everybody. There is even a "slow race"—the slowest horse wins!**

*These mustangs have been tamed. They carry riders on a ranch.*

# Mustangs Today

Free-running horses are found in many parts of the world. But they are not mustangs. Mustangs are found only in North America. Once, America's free-running mustangs were almost gone. They are not out of danger yet. But many people are working to help them. They are working to save places where the mustangs can run. And they are finding homes for mustangs that must be caught. Mustangs running free are a wonderful sight. And they are a big part of America's story. With luck, they will be with us for a long time!

> Australia has more feral horses than anyplace else in the world. Australians call their free-running horses *brumbies*.

> About half of America's free-running mustangs live in Nevada.

*Mustangs are beautiful, powerful horses.*

# Body Parts of a Horse

1. Ears
2. Forehead
3. Forelock
4. Eyes
5. Nostril
6. Muzzle
7. Lips
8. Chin
9. Cheek
10. Neck
11. Shoulder
12. Chest
13. Elbow
14. Forearm
15. Chestnut
16. Knee
17. Cannon
18. Pastern
19. Coronet
20. Hoof
21. Barrel
22. Fetlock
23. Hock
24. Tail
25. Gaskin
26. Stifle
27. Point of hip
28. Croup
29. Loin
30. Back
31. Withers
32. Mane
33. Poll

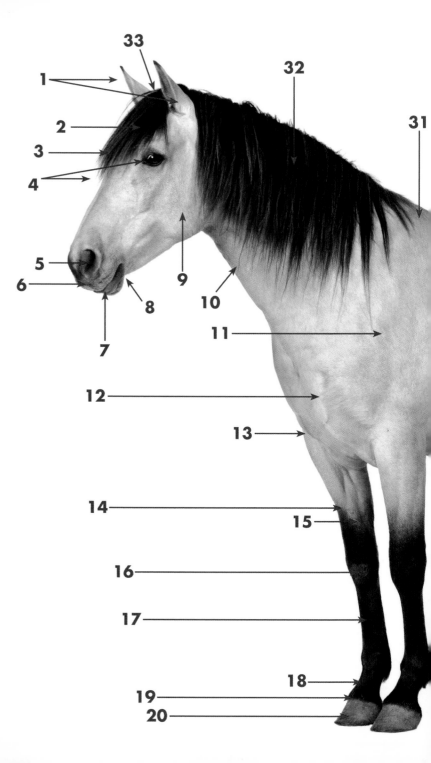

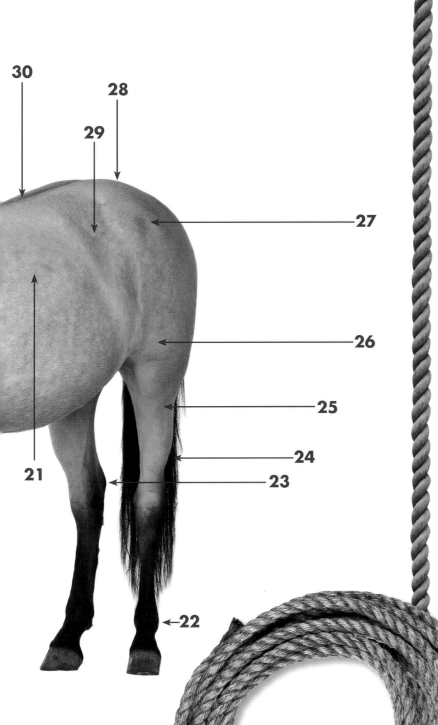

**30**

**28**

**29**

**27**

**26**

**25**

**24**

**21**

**23**

**22**

# To Find Out More

**IN THE LIBRARY**

Budd, Jackie. *The World of Horses*. Boston, Kingfisher, 2004.

Cowley, Joy. *Where Horses Run Free: A Dream for the American Mustang*. Honesdale, PA: Boyds Mills Press, 2003.

Featherly, Jay. *Mustangs: Wild Horses of the American West*. Minneapolis, MN: Carolrhoda, 1986.

Gentle, Victor, and Janet Perry. *Mustangs: America's Wild Horses*. Milwaukee, WI: Gareth Stevens, 1998.

**ON THE WEB**

Visit our Web site for lots of links about Mustangs:
**www.childsworld.com/links**

*Note to Parents, Teachers, and Librarians: We routinely check our Web links to make sure they're safe, active sites—so encourage your readers to check them out!*

# Glossary

**bay (BAY)** A bay horse is brown with a black mane and tail. Many mustangs are bays.

**breeds (BREEDZ)** Breeds are certain types of an animal. Mustangs are a mix of different horse breeds.

**chestnut (CHEST-nut)** A chestnut horse is reddish brown with a brown mane and tail. Many mustangs are chestnuts.

**contests (KON-tests)** In contests, people or animals try to win by being the best at something. Mustangs do well in some kinds of contests.

**dun (DUN)** A dun horse is a grayish yellow color with a black mane and tail. Many mustangs are duns.

**feral (FEHR-ul)** A feral animal is one that has gotten away from its owners and gone wild. Mustangs are feral horses.

**foals (FOHLZ)** Foals are baby horses. Mustangs take good care of their foals.

**mares (MAYRZ)** Mares are female horses. A mustang herd often has several mares.

**roan (ROHN)** Roan horses are a solid color with a few white hairs. Some mustangs are roans.

**stallion (STAL-yun)** A stallion is a male horse. A mustang herd is led by a stallion.

**withers (WIH-thurz)** The withers is the highest part of a horse's back. A mustang's height is measured at the withers.

# Index

adopting, 14, 18

appearance, 7, 8

babies, 4, 13

bay, 8

chestnut, 8

coloring, 8

in contests, 18

dangers to, 13. 14. 17. 18

dun, 8

Europeans, 13

feral, 4, 13, 17, 21

foals, 10

gentling, 18

gymkhana, 18

hands (height), 7

herds, 4, 10, 13

history, 13, 14

hooves, 8

legs, 7, 8

life span, 17

location, 4, 21

mane, 8

mare, 10

name, 4, 7

protection of, 21

roan, 8

scars, 7

stallions, 10

withers, 7

working, 21